My God Smiles

by

Sweet Sparrow
Dr. Nancy Perry Lopes

My God Smiles

Part III

Chapters

Dedication

This book is dedicated to Native American elders, who are also Christian. Our elders, men, and women are not elected or appointed, but are self-proclaimed, admired, respected and spiritually gifted. Elders use knowledge and acumen attained from watching and listening at tribal ceremony and customary festivals. Each then shares ethnic values and principles with tribal members. Essentially, elders are librarians of Native American wisdom, history, and conviction, and believe that the ways of the past are of vital importance to the everyday life of the present and must be preserved into the future.

Elders who are Christian are drawn to serve by God's Holy Spirit and his son's love. These elders are relatively new to Native folklore but invaluable to our tribes. Their wisdom is expansive and divine. Natives have come to accept that Christ thrives in America, not so much as an idea, deity, mood, conviction, or sentiment, but as a commitment or a destiny on a personal level, with eternal implications.

To all elders I humbly bow. And to the worldwide brotherhood of Jehovah's people, I extend much praise, honor, and adulation.

Acknowledgements

I have found the "great peace." What is the "great peace?" Well, peace automatically suggests an absence of war, conflict, or confusion—a time void of negative noise. One bulbous war that I have fought has been spiritual, which is colored by temptation, human frailty, and world conditions. Every day I am faced with its fervidity. And since conflict continuously erupts, even that from within, there are few times in my life when peace existed, especially the "great peace." Removing negatives, both internally and externally is extremely difficult, but when accomplished, even for a short period of time, in flows the "great peace."

I thank those who knowingly and unknowingly have given me access to this peace, such as Jonathan, Jeanine, Leo, Barbara, Manuel, Susan, Dave, now deceased, Eugene, Rebecca, Cora, Charlotte, passed away, Gertrude, Debbie, Minerva, Basilio, also passed, Joe, Rhonda, Peggy, Vera, Jerry, Doris, passed, Gloria, Myra, George, Desiree, Lorise, Betty, Carol, Pat, Marla, Maria, Edith, Charles, Luisita, Juanita, Jacob, Elvin, Nilsa, Sharmone, Miriam, Katie, Linda and Dennis and Aria, Rick who all assisted me in finding the great peace. There are so many more, but these had direct influence. May each of you also find your great peace, always remembering to look for it in God, who smiles on our quests and blesses our efforts. The Great

God of the Universe promises unending peace to humankind, inviting all to partake of his gift of "great peace," both now and forever.

My God Smiles

Chapter 1
Ottucke: Realizing Dreams

"Each human should frame life so that at some future hour fact and dream meet."
Victor Hugo

The year that I stopped working was a year of many changes and realized dreams. I quit all three of my adjunct teaching positions and bought a plane ticket to Puerto Rico. I was tired of waiting for a better future, so I took charge of creating one. When I climbed on the plane, voices in my head were telling me not to go. Without listening, I boarded, looked out of the window, and saw my life being broken up into tiny pieces and released into space. I didn't know what would become of my life, but the not knowing was just fine. When I got to Puerto Rico, the pieces were re-shaped. I spent two weeks with a friend and her sister, found a permanent address before they left, and gasped at my newly forming revitalizations.

During the second week, I was forced to focus on my new surroundings. I saw mountains burning, something that I had never seen before. Smoke was pouring out of the hills, with the wind carrying the smoke down toward the road in undulating sheets. I felt as if the smoke was taking me with it everywhere, comforting me, propelling me, minimizing the time spent in my once hopeless and bored life, changing me, and stretching me out. In fact, the thick smoke immediately settled into the nooks and crannies of my mind. I breathed it in before it dissipated and disappeared into the horizon. For Native Americans, fire and smoke symbolize dreams that live within, dreams that were red-hot and burning up my past. I was visually ablaze with transformation.

Hesitantly, I focused on my dreams. Psychologists believe that every human is born with the capacity to dream. However, much of what we dream is taught. We learn to dream society's dreams. Therefore, our dreams start on the outside and are then internalized. Heredity heartens the dreaming process. The outside dreams come to us from our parents, friends, schools, religions, and many other personal belief systems. What we fuse into our lives become our memories; precisely stored in our minds. The memories control us, causing some to remain dreamers, never realists.

But for me, finally, my dreams were coming true. And my memories were serving as steppingstones into a brighter future. So, I reached into my memories, took out what I wanted and buried the rest. I combined my memories with my dreams and created a new reality. Truly, no dream materializes unless it is cleverly ignited by a memory, so I drip started a clear dream path, opening up a newly sculpted life.

As I looked back, I realized that for many years my dreams laid dormant. However, what you are reading right now is one of my dreams. It is a dream thrice realized. Before writing, I survived by reading the dreams of others and since reading is the act of dreaming with the brain awake, my dreams are now yours.

The mind literally dreams twenty hours a day. So, thus far I have accumulated 752,580 hours of dreams, while still counting. I have dreamed universally, planetarily, continentally, internationally, nationally, tribally, communally, familiarly, and personally. My dreaming is collective and consists of billions of smaller personal considerations, which when viewed publicly; create visions that I am now sharing.

However, sadly, some of my stored memoires are nightmares, which had me holding on tightly to an unhappy life. I didn't know how to let go. And most of the time, I didn't want to let go---for fear of what might come next. What has replaced my stagnation is a desire to erase the past and move into the present. Actually, I looked past the present and into the truth. Truly, mountains of memories majestically landscaped my mind.

I cautiously searched them as though looking for a penny dropped into a wishing well. I allowed my memories to climb through thickly folded brain tissue. Many were locked away, but are now breaking free, like paint peeling off a shabby building. Many are like morning mist, often released without warning. However, in my search for truth, justice, love, and success, I've realized that I was living a life of lies, wretchedness and stagnation. I dreamed of release. no longer wanting to listlessly live my life in the shadow of the dreams of others, with no light projected on my foremothers, my parents, my marriage, my gender, or myself.

Sorrow was hosted by me, sucking my energy, without any useful return. The unhappiness stung. Then, I destroyed the parasite, once and for all, and gained control. When the old me died, the parasite died too. It took great courage and God's love to change. However, by giving up the past, I am enjoying the present. I have no time for self-pity. The more I develop self-love, the less I accept abuse.

Timidly, I have mustered up a certain amount of personal power, and I am now rebuilding my life. By stepping out of the shadows, and into the beauty of unfiltered light, I am grounding myself in constructive self-realization, taking hold of who I am, who I want to be, and who God wants me to be. My mind and heart are actualizing my aspirations. I am a new me.

The beauty of coming to this point in life, is that I no longer wonder why the one that I loved did not treat me lovingly. In fact, I view his treatment as a gift. He gifted me with singleness. Without him, I anticipate no further years of despair. When he released me, I was hurt, but my heart continues to heal. His gift allows me new life choices. And I am now happy, single, and free.

I found that there is no greater happiness than letting go of your past and seeing your possibilities. Yes, I have had a long history of heartache, that I have painfully navigated through. However, my memories also contain granules of sweetness that neither time nor circumstance can sour.

That January, I promised myself that I would live out the conclusion of my days happy and in peace. Rather than being bitter, I have become more loving, more grateful, and more in control of the direction of my life. Whatever life takes away from me, I let go. Being true to myself helps me to reject the voices that used to misguide me. Instead, I hear the voice of God distinctly and directly.

Hence, in just five short weeks in Puerto Rico, my life became productive. I had a new apartment, a new car, new friends, but most importantly, a new life. The negative noise in my past dissolved into the tides of the sea. I am now fulfilling my dreams, loving my family, satisfying my tribal duties, and honoring and worshiping my God. I have learned from my mistakes, looked honestly at my past and moved forward.

I now have the courage to take on meaningful challenges. I cannot truthfully say that I have found everything that I am looking for, but I have chosen to stand firm in my Nativity, my womanhood, and my faith. I am living a space between what is and what will be, without judgment, victimization, gossip, or exploitation.

And I thank God every day for the gifts he gives and for showing me that I have everything that I have ever truly needed. I finally love my life. Gosh, it only took five decades, and observing the fires burning on my new island home to enlighten me. My reality is serene, no longer hidden, and no longer pushing my purpose for living into anonymity. I am living with the great peace.

Chapter 2
Sitala: Sharing the Memories

*"The great `tragedy in life is not death. It is to stop laughing, stop **loving,
dreaming: stopping** everything while yet still alive." Oscar Wilde*

For much of my life, memories gave me many reasons to cry. They often crept into my heart, slipped out of my eyes, and roll down my cheeks. Now I record them to be shared and compared. Comparing memories facilitates growth—for the bearer and the sharer. And truly, sharing my heart costs nothing. Many of my memories are painful, but they contribute to my uniqueness. In fact, my life has been guided by a compass of memories, all pointing me to where I am today. I have learned to navigate through the multitude of memories, both good and bad, in order to survive.

My first memory is of mother, when I was six months old. I see a beautiful Native woman. She is sitting on a chair holding and feeding me a bottle of warm milk. Her unbound hair is flowing like dark water, spilling down behind her like a voluminous waterfall. Her soulful jet-black eyes carry the sorrows of our tribe, her life, and the lives of her children, and yet, also radiate love. Smiling down at me, she softly says, "I love you, my *papoose.* And I feel her love, devotion, and protection, never wanting to leave her arms or the intensity of her adoring gaze, knowing that her love would last forever.

A mother's love is a beautiful treasure. Mother was not a woman who often displayed her love tactically, but I always knew it was there, that day and every day thereafter. Mother has long since passed away, but the memory of her love continues in my heart. Every now and then a piece of her life and love tears away from me and floats across the forever horizon. I have lost her, but never her love. Nothing kills a mother's love.

Years passed and when I turned eleven, I understood how hard life was for mother. She was forced to be our mother and our father, frequently finding the jobs overwhelming. So often in her duality, her love was marred by distress, which caused her and her loved ones much pain and agony. Mother lived much of her own life unloved. Wanting what was best for us, she demanded exclusive observance of her design. When we deviated, we were severely chastised.

Mother's form of discipline was extreme and harsh, learned from her Native parents. They and she sought to break the spirits of their children, all succeeding at times. In fact, every so often mother's discipline was uncontrolled and administered with twisted, degrading, and cruel abhorrence.

The duplicity of her behavior caused me to both love and fear her. Fearing her, produced in me a personality confused about love and later life. By then she was severely tying her rich black hair back from her pretty, but sadly sullen face. Her love was sparse, like overlapping ringlets of mane on the nape of the neck of an animal. And her eyes were encircled in redness from her many hours of shedding tears. The love I remembered was replaced with rage. She was emotionally and physically austere, almost void of warmth and feeling, loveless and in continual anguish.

At twelve, mother's love became regulatory. She spoke not with words, but with her unforgiving and abusive hands. Mother touched me un-lovingly, showing no affection or comfort. I knew she loved me, but she punctuated it with cruelty. In my bewilderment, I endured her brutality and later saw myself becoming like her. When I imitated her unwholesome antics, I created disaster in my own life.

Oh, how I wish I had been loved without harshness. In fact, if I could have patterned after the mother of my first memory, a richer bond with my children would have resulted. However, by eighteen I was mother, not the Native woman I would have liked to be. Still and all, I am eternally grateful for mother's quiet courage, fierce stoicism, and staunch resilience. She was the woman that her life created, the one that produced me.

I know that father, a ruthless, domestically violent Native man also added to mother's change. I remember father beating mother at least three or four times a year. When he beat her, he appeared strong, although now I understand that beating a woman is an act of cowardice, not strength. Adding to the violence, he was a binge drunk, a functional alcoholic, a genetic trait of Natives. He went to work Monday through Friday and to bars Friday night through Sunday evening.

Father worked nights during the week, and on Sunday nights, he sometimes went to work drunk. Mother prepared a thermos of hot black coffee to get him through the night, but he, also a diabetic (another trait of Native Americans), often fell asleep on the job. Once when I was thirteen, father was fired for sleeping at work and for coming to work in a drunken stupor. When he came home late one Monday morning, he spoke with deep resonance while his black eyes projected internal hurt. He had spent the better part of that morning begging to be reinstated to his job, and succeeded, but lost his manhood in the process.

Father too is deceased, but I remember him as a man who proudly proclaimed his ethnicity. However, when he was fired and later reinstated, he swallowed his indigenous smugness. He was never the same after that. In his humiliation, he lost his Native dignity, his inner self respect, and his own fulsome heart. He no longer drank after that experience, and never again expressed his manhood brutally, but he lost far too much. He lost his wife, his house and the respect of his kids. No job is worth such sacrifice, and no man should have to endure such defeat.

Father, always a man of few words, who, after the degradation, spoke less and less. He lost what he worked so hard to gain; and we lost his witty barbs and his measured love. It was as if father's world ended in a wide-open space that swallowed him alive. I hated to see how necessity broke him, leaving him in his puniness. Nonetheless, I thankfully adopted his pride of ethnicity before he unjustly lost it.

Yes, I have found my place in the world of words and in the communication of memories. Words express thoughts spoken or written, good or bad, earmarking all with meaning. I record even the most damning memories as significant, knowing that memories bind people and families together. They create a unity that cannot be broken. Once created, memories recorded and shared solidify the past and expand the possibilities of the future. When I record thoughts, freedom drips down my spine and onto the pages of many books. The words keep flowing.

The way a family, a tribe, a race, a nation lives on, is through sharing of memories, in communicative styles that like shooting stars, pull everything around them into ever-expanding vortex of forever. My family is Native American, a penetrating people who have been as pervasive as salt, and as insurgent. We are confrontational, but that has not destroyed our comradery. Like any other Native family, we can imaginatively look out into a distant purple haze to see great tall tepees, campfires, grazing horses, children playing and the love of family and tribe in abundance. Yes, this my heritage and will become my legacy.

Chapter 3
Wa'ba nang: Retirement

"Life begins at retirement." Author Unknown

In the 2010 Census, 2.4 million people in the US were identified as American Indian and Alaska Native, either alone or in combination with one or more other races. I fall into the Native/Alaskan/African American category at 269,421 persons, comprising 0.1 percent of the population. Of that number, less than $1/10^{th}$ of 0.1 percent is now living in retirement. However small the number, my Native life in retirement is just beginning.

The truth is, I looked forward to retirement. I knew that I did not want to return to the poverty from whence I came. But before retiring, there was hardly time to wonder about the future because the present was so demanding. Nevertheless, when I stopped working, it felt right. I worked for four- and one-half decades and knew that it was time to stop. And in just over 2½ years in retirement, I feel physically and mentally exhilarated. I am not adrift, depressed, or forlorn. I am doing something millions of American workers dream about doing someday, which is living the life of leisure. I thank God and Social Security for this time.

Even so, transitioning into retirement was at first tough. According to psychologists, jobs provide mental health benefits that afford balance and stability. Without my job, I tried not to fear the prospect of days upon months upon years of clock less

free time. I did not think of retirement only in terms of subtraction, as the eliminating

of the responsibilities of a job and purpose. Nor I did enter a vacuum or a new cos-

mos. Instead, I slowed down and then moved on.

I got off the treadmill, out of the grind, planned to do nothing for a while, and

began to create a new me. Still and all, at first, the inactivity was rather depressing

because of lessened "perception" and cognitive processing. As an educator, I know

that the brain is like any other muscle. So, with less use, I was without intellectual

stimulation. With time I became a little more successful in retirement because I de-

vised a plan for what to do with my days and life of reduced finances.

I realized that I couldn't view retirement with "a vacation mentality." Granted,

I had to restructure my identity and live with less, knowing that statistics suggest

that on average a person can live for about twenty years after retirement. I decided

not to feel "empty, purposeless, aimless, or poor, and put a twenty-year plan into

practice, telling myself, "You are going to enjoy this phase of your life because you

deserve it."

As a Native professional woman, part of my identity was very much tied to my

paycheck. However, as an educator, I found myself more susceptible to a rougher transition from workplace to retirement, because I had worked collectively with others, and had to learn to work alone. Additionally, I had become very accustomed to people needing me, and it is quite addicting to feel essential. Moving to Puerto Rico eased the "I am needed" crisis, because having separated from the family, job, and tribe erased my previous interactions.

However, it was hard to accept the sudden separation from daily contact with workplace friends, colleagues, family, tribal representatives, and media associates. So, I spent a lot of time sleeping. The matter of filling a large chunk of time each day seemed to be beyond me. Time is one of the world's deepest mysteries. It can be likened to a wind that never stops. To be quite honest, I was grieving my losses. Days were passing with my life in a state of suspension like one elongated note in a symphony. The tune playing was morose, somewhat sad and sickening, and I didn't know how to change it.

I felt worthless and missed the routines, the responsibilities, and the satisfaction that I gained from doing my job well for so long a period of time. Subsequently, I gave in to nothingness. Then I realized that I had to regroup. I wanted to be retired and I wanted to enjoy the rest of my life.

Having moved to Puerto Rico, I began to learn about the new culture. I didn't want to socially isolate, so I made new friends. All the while, the Caribbean sun was spilling over me like molten gold, indicative of the island's name. Delightfully, I learned to appreciate my new environment, while becoming physically and mentally healthier.

I am enjoying retirement largely because I have created a new innocuous identity. When I taught my last class, I closed off a large portion of my life. I had been living to please others, which was one of the reasons I chose to become a teacher. Now I teach ten Bible studies on a weekly basis. I am passionate in my teaching and have settled into being a minister, a mother, and friend. I don't have to tout academic degrees or job titles to be heard, I simply teach. Teaching has always been my life but no longer defines me. However, it does still bring me joy. I used to identify myself by my profession and allowed my career to control my life. Now I am liberated. It took about six months to review, reflect, reconcile, and accept the new direction of my life, and with new shallow breathing I am settled into retirement.

I live in the moment of each breath in the span of time between an inhale and an exhale. My new breathing pattern has brought me new knowledge and understanding. I am wiser now. Without the burden of a daily job, I have time to collect and consider the memories of the past, people of influence, events of significance and places of impression. Retirement allows me to recognize my accomplishments, understand and forgive my perceived failures, and to set a new course for the rest of my life.

Wisdom is guiding my life choices. And my life is now rich and immersive. I have come a long way, finally finding a semblance of peace. Will Rogers once said, "Half our life is spent trying to find something to do with the time we have rushed through life trying to save." I have learned to appreciate "the moment" and to "wait for the right time."

I love my retirement and its positivity. My heart exalts in tranquility, peace, and serenity. I have been blessed by the choices I made and continue to make. When I was young, I didn't realize how my choices would pan out. And still I have zillions of choices to be made. Being the master of my own ship, I have allowed this life of retirement to put a chuckle in every utterance coming forth from my mouth. My retired brain cells have lit up, like a freshly changed light bulb. God, retirement, and wisdom are great. *Wa'ba nang,* to all, which is the Native American word for retirement.

Chapter 4
Onawa: My Daughter Leaves Home

"First my daughter forever my friend." Anonymous

My daughter is tantamount to my new life. The mother-daughter relationship is one of the strongest and most complex bonds in the world. It is considered one of the most powerful connections in nature that only mothers and daughters understand and share. For Native mothers and daughters this bond is tribally fortified. Tribal mothers teach their daughters to stand strong. My mother taught me the rudiments of personal and tribal survival, and I taught my daughter.

The knowledge that Native mothers transmit to their daughter is essential to the redemption or survival of our threatened and endangered nations. Like my mother with me, I provided cultural underpinnings, insulating her from the corrosive effects of her non-Native environment. "What has happened to many Native nations, we must attempt to curtail," I said. She listened intently. I taught my daughter what I know, and later in life she re-educated me.

Sadly, however, I never quite learned how to nurture my daughter properly, thus, she suffered from low self-esteem. Often, she appeared naive and innocent to life's travesties. She did, however, object to the abuses that I failed to reject, and over the years I have seen her grow into a love of life and of herself. She observed how for years I lowered a veil over my life, a black fog of forgetfulness, so impenetrable that as the years passed, I fooled myself into believing that none of what I lived ever happened. She forced me to face the truth.

In doing so, we were often in conflict, with differing opinions, finding that our disagreements resulted in more connection than disconnection. However, we have supplanted the mother-daughter dyad with a sister-sister relationship, coming to understand that Native woman always stick together, as we have.

The bridge of continuity for Native women is preserved in the embedding of cultural values, our shared past, and individual and collective identities of self and tribe. I poured into my daughter the fundamentals of our Nativity by giving her small methodical sips of our culture, even though she often wanted to take instantaneous gulps.

She also wanted to find her own place in society, without me, and without my cultural nudging. But at the end of each day, she was always there to comfort and strengthen me while I faced the cruelties that were part of my life. We became a fortuitous team.

A mother's treasure is her daughter. And unlike my marriage, ours was a bond that I felt could never be broken. My daughter felt the same way. I thought that even when my daughter found a man, it would simply mean that then we would be three.

Still and all, my daughter left me on two separate occasions. The first time she left was for about one month when she was eighteen. She wanted to stop attending our kingdom hall and knew that such a decision would be a grave point of contention in our home. She wanted religious freedom. Rather than enter such a battle, she left. She went to live in the home of a woman who had just been baptized as one of Jehovah's Witnesses. I knew that this new living arrangement would be short lived, so I waited for my daughter to come to her senses and allowed her space to grow.

The newly baptized mother told my daughter, "You are not free to leave God in my home." She made my daughter so miserable that she called me within a month to come and help her move her belongings out of the home of the woman and back into our home. I was not only relieved but overjoyed. Lessons in life often come with adverse consequences, and my daughter got a bitter taste of reality. After that bout with freedom, she remained in my home until she was twenty-seven. During those years, she kept weaving in and out of her relationship with God, as she is still doing even to this day.

When she settled on a mate, she told me, "When I get married you are going to have to find your own way." Next, she told me, "Leo and I are planning to move to Arizona for a job that has been offered to him. What are you going to do?" How could my daughter even think about leaving me? I swallowed the hurt that rose like heartburn. Mothers and daughters," I reasoned, "are forever." What happened to her and me?

At night, I would lay on my bed like a broken doll. My heart was further fragmented. I moved through life listlessly. She, her fiancé, and I shared my home for about a year, and then I felt that I could no longer live so unhappily. I wrote to the US Branch Office of Jehovah's Witnesses and asked where a single older sister could best serve to promote kingdom growth. I was guided to the Island of Puerto Rico. Without hesitation, I made plans to move. I was petrified. But I became a heroine in my own story instead of waiting for one to come along. I shocked my daughter, but most of all I shocked me. Then, I was gone.

It has now been over two years since I left. I miss my daughter more than I miss anyone else. I miss our closeness and our bond of love. Sure, we have never gotten to the point of understanding each other, and yesterday, my daughter said to me,

"Don't get mad, but I have never really respected you for running." I didn't get mad, instead I told her that I had no other choice.

I love my daughter with all my heart, and I respect her not just because it is my obligation, but because I value her place in our Native continuum. Without my strong daughter, there could be no Native tomorrow. Her strength will drive our tribal nation into the next generation, and my teachings will flow through her body by way of blood, exceedingly hot, all the way to the stream source---our unfailing love.

Chapter 5
Tiyata: Finding a Home

"If you go anywhere, even paradise, you will miss your home."
Malaya Yousafzai

I left everything in my apartment just the way that I wanted to find it when I returned. I told myself that I was leaving forever, but I knew that I would one day return. When I finally did return, I found out that it was not the apartment that I missed, but it was my family. The word family suggests warmth, working together, common goals, growth, love, and happiness. My real sense of security was lost, not because of the apartment, but because I had lost the love that only family can provide. Somehow, I felt that if I left and came back then I would find "home," which is sometimes synonymous with family. Family has everything to do with blood, and home has everything to do with heart. The day I returned, my heart was saying out loud, "Did you know that home and family are the nicest words that can be uttered?"

Over the years I have lived in many houses, and I can recall all of them. Each structure I called home, but for the most part, there has always been something missing. In none of them resided a happy family. And to none of them did I ever want to return.

My first house was at 200 Blackstone Street in Providence, Rhode Island. It was a structure built in the 1800s, with two full apartments, a basement, and attic. Our family lived on the first floor and no one lived on the second. It was warm and cheerful, but for my mother it was never a home. Mother hated the location, the mice and the neighborhood. She often complained to my father and he did everything that he could on his meager salary to move mother out.

We moved to 327 Blackstone Street, just up the block. The house was bigger, the neighborhood was more secure, but the house was still not home to mother. This house also had two tenements, an attic and a cellar. This time we lived on the second floor. I loved this house. It was all that I believed that we needed to be a happy family, and I have many found memories of the house. I shared a bedroom with my brother and my sisters shared a dining room that we used as their bedroom. I played often on our porch and there was a space in the backyard that brother and I called our playground. Father had a garage for his car and I had a tree that allowed me to get on top of the garage, which I used as a hidden refuge.

What mother did not like about the house was that it was infested with rats, cockroaches, and sat beside the house of a neighbor drug user. On the weekends, my extended family members came to sit on our porch to see what the drug user and the drunkards would do when high. However, since mother was deathly afraid of rodents, she complained to the landlady often---so much that the relationship between the landlady and our family became strained. The landlady avoided mother because mother constantly confronted her about exterminating the house. Little did we know that the whole neighborhood was infested, and extermination would have been not only a waste of money, but futile. So, mother kept begging father to get us out of that neighborhood, and after five years of mother's complaints, he did.

We moved to Warwick, Rhode Island. Father purchased a plot of land and with the help of a moonlight construction worker that he met at his job; they built mother a new house. It was located at 177 Vernon Street. It had three bedrooms, a kitchen, a living room and a bathroom, a basement, and an attic crawl space. It was about 1200 square feet in size, tiny, but it was the first house that mother called home. There were no mice, rats, cockroaches, druggies, or alcoholics. For the first time, mother seemed to be happy in her home. We were on top of each other all the time, but because we were teens, much of our time was spent out of the house, so we persevered. I believe we endured based on mother's happiness and then we got to a point when father could no longer afford it.

Mother did all that she could to save her home. She even got a job at a nursing home so that she could help father pay the bills. The irony in her getting a job is that she did help pay the bills, but she also met a man who convinced her to leave her home and to move to Providence with him. So much for finding happiness in a structure of wood and cement. When mother left, I never felt happy within those Warwick walls again. I never felt at home in mother's Providence location either. I felt homeless and since I was then in my first year of college, I began staying on the campus during the summers or going on extended vacations to make up for my displacement. Homeless is not a happy state.

Once, my college roommate and I went to Long Beach, California for a summer. She was going for adventure; I went in search of a place to call home. My godmother was living in a house in Long Beach by herself and I thought that maybe I could move in with her and have a home. That plan fell through and back to my state of homelessness I went. I remained that way for the next three years. In fact, I was just as displaced as my Native ancestors had been, while I was going to school on my father's tribal land. How ironic.

After completing my undergraduate degree, I moved to New York and into the home of a college friend. He was planning to do graduate work in Rhode Island, and I was planning graduate work in New York. In his guilt for not moving back to New York with his parents, he suggested that I take his place in his parents' home. I lasted in that Brooklyn apartment for only two days. I don't even remember its address, but I do remember my unhappiness there. A high school friend was living with her boy-friend in the Bronx and suggested that we get an apartment together in Manhattan where she worked. We found my fourth residence, a cute one-bedroom apartment at 276 East 90th Street.

I loved our little apartment. It was small with a pantry like kitchen, a tiny bath-room, living room, and bedroom. There was no light, no air, and no space, but it felt like home. I would still be living there had it not been for the fact that my roommate got another boyfriend who thought that it was funny to lay around the house naked and to touch my roommate in private places at any time of the day or night. I became uncomfortable in our apartment, and it no longer felt like home. My roommate sensed my discomfort and moved out.

Not able to afford the rent alone, I moved too. My roommate moved to West 85th Street. She told me about an apartment on the street that was for rent. I went to see the apartment and fell in love with it. It was modern, large, and comfortable. I felt like I had finally found my home. This apartment was located at 315 West 85th Street. It was a duplex with the bedroom and bathroom on the bottom level with lots of light and space. The top floor was the kitchen and living room. I could not afford the apartment by myself, so I posted signs on my Columbia University campus and got a new roommate in a few days. We both loved the apartment, the location and each other. My new roommate did, however, decide to move when my boyfriend started to spend weekends at our place. After she left, my boyfriend and I began to live together so that I could afford what I was calling my home.

We stayed at that location for about one year, and then the apartment was burglarized. I feared that neighborhood and that location, and since my high school friend had moved to Riverdale, New York, I asked her to find an apartment for us there. She found an apartment for us at 512 Kapppock Street and my boyfriend and I moved in. Riverdale sits right on the Hudson River so there was a breeze and a view. We couldn't see much from our first-floor apartment, but it was airy and spacious. This time I had a large living room, a small dining room, a kitchen, a large bedroom, and a large bathroom. The apartment had ceiling to floor windows and lots of greenery and flowers. I thought again, maybe this is finally home, so I began purchasing large items of furniture, even a piano. This time I thought I was grounded, but my boyfriend didn't like being in such a remote location, so he kept returning to Manhattan. With him gone so much, my new apartment became a prison for me, not a home.

By that time, we were engaged, so we looked for a place that we could purchase. We found a starter home in Monroe, New York, a three-bedroom single family structure with less space than our Kappock Street apartment. I wanted the house to work for us, to become our home. My husband had a pool table on one side of the two-car garage, and the entire bottom floor of the bi-level for himself. He and I seemed to be happy there. We got married had both of our children in that house and then he walked out. I was devastated. Our house was not a home after all.

He returned, and we again conducted a search for the happy home. We were by that time running a small day care business and I got the bright idea to buy a large house which could be used as our business and our home. We found a 6,000-square foot house with three floors and a full basement. It sat on three acres, had a two-car garage, an in-ground pool with a jacuzzi, a full two-story barn, and a work shed. Finally, I found our "home," or so I felt.

I remember telling my mother-in-law that we would never have to move again. I really believed those words until my marriage disintegrated and the house that I loved and shared with my family for over twenty-five years, was no longer my happy home. Other than my 327 Blackstone Street home in Providence, this home was the closest thing to happiness that I had found. I have fond memories and many stories, but it was in this location that I learned that it is not a structure that makes a home; instead, it is the love and comradery of family that does.

I planned to leave that house too. I put the house on the market and chose a family that said they would rent it with an option to buy. My daughter and I found a beautiful apartment of some 2,500 square feet in Nyack, New York. Again, we fell in love with the space and believed it too could become our new home. My daughter and I set out to beautifully furnish our new apartment and to start our family life afresh. The apartment and the location were appropriate for a new beginning.

In the new space, I got to clearly see my spouse. He was aloof and I became bereft. Determining how many houses I had lived in throughout my life, I finally realized that a house, without a happy family, is not a home.

I silently traveled over the mountains in my mind, and the valleys in my heart, even spent a great deal of time on the borders of my seclusion. I came to realize that I needed to leave Nyack in search of a place that I could call home. And very quickly, in another country, I found one that was fire engine red. To my liking my new living space soothed my troubled soul. Still, I didn't feel as if it was truly home. When I entered my house, I would always say, "Welcome home." I was happy within my walls, and my house swelled with good cheer, but was it my home?

In less than one year, I found myself again searching for another place. I was lonely. Love didn't reside with me. My heart yearned for home. I finally realized that loneliness is like the horizon. Wherever you go it meets you. To foil my loneliness, I moved again and found a house with two bedrooms. I thought that I could get my children and possibly my husband to come to Puerto Rico to visit me. For six months, no one came, so I planned to go and see them. As soon as I purchased my ticket, both of children called to say they were coming. It was too late. I was already in motion, heading home. Yes, I was heading home, but I had no idea as to what I would find there. Was home now looking for me?

As I traveled back to the states, I let go of my loneliness virtually one mile at a time. My need to see my family fluttered merrily like a pennant in the wind. I was going to arrive in the dead of a dreadful New England winter, so I flew west first. I spent two months in California before heading to the east coast and snow. When I arrived in February, swirling snow, soft as cotton, danced gaily in the wind. I arrived at Boston's Logan Airport and was met by my son and a limousine driver. There was an air of happiness, because I was heading to the home that my son lived in--- the home of my deceased parents. I took off my coat and my boots and set merrily, full of newly discovered content. I stayed for months with my son, my daughter, and my two sisters and then I decided to return to Puerto Rico, only this time to a new location.

I now live in Culebra. It is an island paradise with beautiful trade winds and breath-taking beaches. I try not to live in houses that look tired; those with cracking paint, missing clapboards, or damaged doors. It reminds me of the houses in my past that I could never call home.

And no, I have not found home, because I now know that home is not a place. I have stopped searching for home, because for the most part, I am alone. I now look at my existence like the setting of the sun contemplating its decent in the reflection it sees in the sea. Culebra, for me. is a quiet space in my mind. It is a slit in time where I have chosen to hide. My thoughts now come to me freely, as if they have loomed over the horizon for years. No, Culebra is not home, but for now it is the place where I have chosen to shed so many years of pain. In Culebra, my worry lines have smoothed out on my face.

No, Culebra is not home, but it is a place where my quest to find it has stopped. I have no distinct home, but I do have a family and I love them. In my love for them, I have found the true meaning of home. Home is the place where family comes together, even if this does not happen in one specific structure. Native Ameicans say that if you take a bunch of sticks, light each one on fire, separate them, the whole bunch goes out. However, when you put them all together again and relight the bundle, it will burn hotly----that is what home is. I know that whenever my family is together, that place can be called home.

Chapter 6
Ina aopemni inajinpi: The Children Want Mates

"Mating may be Nature's provision for maintaining the balance of the species." P.G.   Wodehouse

Nevertheless, no one wants to be alone. I have always known that humans were created with the need to love and to be loved. This is a proper desire. And mating requires universal eugenics. Humans and animals exercise a deliberate mating instinct. By natural or personal selection, progeny are produced. And centuries from now, humans will still be mating, marrying, procreating, and perpetuating the species. However, words, even the best combinations, often fall short of a description of finding a suitable mate. The Bible states that the second greatest relationship that any human can have is to love another human being. The love of God is the first.

For Native Americans and Western civilization, it is customary for a person to personally choose a marriage mate. In contemporary Native societies, the mating scene is a familiar one: dinner, movies, dancing, and conversation. But things were vastly different 100 years ago. A vignette entitled, "Lakota Courting Scene," which can be viewed in the Museum of Natural History, Alcoa Foundation Hall of the American Indians shows how young couples connected in tribal societies in the 19th century.

When a young man's thoughts turned to choosing a bride, he needed several accessories-chief among them was a courting blanket, often made for him by his sister. There was no mistaking the intentions of a well-turned-out young man with a blanket draped over his arm, who headed for the tipi of an eligible young woman. Wrapping the blanket around himself and his intended, the man provided a private place for the two to talk. The custom was called *ina aopemni inajinpi*, or "standing wrapped in the blanket," and while its origin is uncertain, scholars do know that it flourished until young people began going away to reservation assigned boarding schools, where mating rituals of Western civilization were adopted.

Blanket wrapping is so old that probably none today actually experienced it, but Natives are aware of it as a charming part of our history. The details are kept alive through oral tradition and through ledger drawings, scenes of daily tribal life, depicted on Native family records obtained from settlers, in trading posts, and at inter-ethnic gathering places.

Native artist, Thomas Red Owl Haukaas, drew a picture of three suitors-two waiting their turn while the first converses with a popular girl. The men wore their finest clothes and beaded moccasins. One even carried an umbrella, both fashionale and practical a century ago. It too was used to insure privacy. The men's hair is carefully groomed, something their sisters often did for them on these special occa-sions, and their skin is decorated with vermillion body paint. And if a fellow needs some additional help, a courting flute is brought for serenading. On this instrument the Native man played songs believed to be irresistible to a young woman and com-posed by a shaman according to instructions received in a dream.

In playing a love song on the courting flute, the suitor emulated a male deer that bugles to lure a mate in his direction. Young Native men were aware of that animal's success in attracting females and they hoped to supernaturally harness a bit of the deer's seductive powers. Additionally, the suitors carried love charms made from deer horn, wore clothing decorated with images of the animal, or adorned their flutes with drawings of deer during the deer's mating process.

The psychology of mating is like the ecology of the sea, the wind, the sand, and the earth. Each depends on the fragile bond that holds the ecosystems together. Mat-ing needs the dependencies of love, trust, and faith. Both of my children have dis-covered that happiness is much more than a feeling. Many positive actions must be carried out by each prospective mate.

And happy people do not find one perfect person to love. Often many are found and left. However, a happy person is one who has found a way to truly love---amid human imperfections. There is no perfect partner and there is no ideal mate. Each discovered that happiness does not come from a suitable mate; instead, it consists of working on creating personal happiness, with or without one.

I would love to see each of my children with a fitting mate. They know that when finding a mate, it is wise to look for the good in the other person and to consider the weaknesses or failures as well. I taught my children that we don't always get who we deserve; oftentimes we get who we need. They know that to develop a close relationship with someone, there must first be understanding of oneself. A good relationship is more an act of will than an uncontrollable result of circumstance. When a person mates with a cheerful and energetic person, there is always an interchange of optimism.

Mating, they know, is a matter of the heart. And the heart is the total of the interior being. They also know that it is wise to peer regularly into the heart, because such a search engenders conditions that result in true peace and prosperity. "To be a good mate," I told my children, "each of you should be a person who is quick to forgive and willing to look for ways to compliment another person's life." Sharing the blanket so to speak.

While both of my children are still in search of the ideal mate, they have come to accept that failure is a symptom and does not have to be the condition of their lives. Since we are all unfinished portraits, there is always a place to add another face. Yes, my children are still in search of mates, that I am certain they will find. Their searches gurgle forward on their journeys to eternal bliss. But most importantly, I want to always choose to share my children's lives over making my own, so I will continue to be there with them as they remain on the hunt.

Chapter 7
Hi-disho: Disenchantment

"It dropped so low that I heard it hit the ground. Then it went to pieces on the stones, at the bottom of my mind." Emily Dickerson

We are all okay, but sometimes in my elder years, I descend back into despair. Since I have been disheartened so often in my life, I must have passed some of my ill will on to my daughter I   My philosophy has been that there is (or ought to be) a remedy (preferably quick and easy) for every unfulfilled longing. I've tried just about everything that I can think of to fix the erraticism in my life, hoping for viable change. I ask for no help and get no affirmation. I simply trudge along waiting for the discontent to disappear or get better. Neither happens. So, I accept what life has given be and move on.

As I stumble though my life, I have identified my longings and have tried to do whatever is necessary to get my "needs" met. I shout out my longings, while others voice theirs. I've always wanted a happy family, peace, and a good relationship with God. So far I've gotten two out of three, and in all honesty, I know that isn't bad. And fortunately, what I have been able to control is my integrity, which means a whole lot to me and is what pulls me through.

So, this part of my story is simple: there is something called enchantment that 1) I never had, but 2) for some reason I thought that I lost. And what I thought that I lost could not be retrieved but for me is still something very valuable. Finding enchantment has been one of my life goals, and I believe that along with it comes joy.

However, I still live with unfulfilled longings. Surely, I get some wants met, only not always when needed. I have done a lot with my life, and I appreciate that. I moved to a paradise island, traveled whenever and wherever, written several books, and raised two kids. Now what I crave most is seeing my family happy and at peace.

Consequently, I continue searching for the truth that can set me free from the bondage of my own deception. I don't want to add another twenty years to my life only to become more disappointed by the things that I haven't attained, so I have sailed away from my safe harbor to explore, dream, and discover. There is no perfect life, marriage, job, or friendship, but there is a universal desire for happiness. And while I am content, I believe that life owes me and those whom I love, much more.

Sadly, my truth has been that for the most part, other humans and inanimate cherished items have consistently disappointed me. Things can burn or break or be stolen or get lost. People can move or change or fail or die. And it took the loss of my marriage some years ago to awaken me to the truth that I may always live in a state of disappointment if I keep looking to people or things to satisfy me.

I do still long for what I do not have, but I am learning to emancipate myself from the bondage of disenchantment. I know now that life is not always fulfilling, and I accept the unfulfilled portions. I still seek, find, enjoy, reinvent, develop, and most importantly share my fulfillment with those who mean the most to me; and I have courageously faced my disenchantment and moved forward undauntingly.

I chose not to be blinded by the truth, stymied by my fears, because I have hurled them into the wind until I am ready to explain or reject them. As I live my life, I promise myself to find it charming, delightful, and enrapturing, which by the way is the definition of enchantment. I refuse to lament the wasted years or to close myself off from enjoying the coming years. I have figured out that enchantment is not so unlikely after all---that it is one of the purest forms of happiness and doesn't require an incubation period, but blooms instantly and readily coloring everything that it touches. May it come soon to me and mine.

Chapter 8
Wicasa, Dayden: Grandchildren

"Grandchildren are the dots that connect the lines from generation to generation." Lois Wyse

Now here is the joy of my life, my grandson. And what I love most is that I am a positive role model for him. Becoming his paragon started with looking in the mirror, and then back to see better what is ahead. I do not want the past to be lost and forgotten or the future to be less certain for him than it need be. And I believe with all my heart that I have been blessed with a boy who looks up to me every day.

As a Native, *tota,* grandma, I want him to have a connection to his roots. With an understanding of his heritage, his future is clear, assured, and full of positivity. Statistics show that more children have less contact with their grandparents than was the case some fifty years prior. That is not the case with us. We spend time together every day. And although my grandson is growing up in a world much different from mine, I am taking the time to understand and teach him how to respond to his difficult challenges. I am helping him to plan for his future with the help of his parents. It is a joint venture of caring and coaching.

Although there are some differences in his parents' styles, there are guidelines and boundaries that all of us live with and mutually respect, even with changing times and generational variation. His mother and I have similar experiences, but our styles of nurturing are different. His father is his playmate and talking buddy. However, all of us bring our uniqueness, including culture, ethnicity, age, race, family traditions, abilities, and personal histories together for his benefit.

My input is exclusive, because I bring age. We learn a lot from each other. Sometimes being an only child and a product of his parent's divorce has been difficult for him, but he has learned how to cope. There is no perfect family or circumstances, so he has learned to accept the duplicity of what he has.

I am the go between for him. Researchers who study grand parenting have identified various styles. These styles include family historian/living ancestor, the nurturer, the mentor, the role model, the playmate, the wizard, and the hero. I have been all of these to my grandson. As the family historian, I share the stories about Native relatives, important events, family traditions, my own childhood, and our inimitable culture. From my stories, my grandson is gaining a positive image of aging and his place in family lineage. The enlightenment I give him is like a lantern on the stern. It shines best on the waves behind. And throughout his short life, I've gotten to provide inspiration and valuable reassurance to him and his parents.

Whether I serve as the babysitter, the chauffeur, the nurse, the confidante, or the caregiver, my challenge has been to find a delicate balance between help and control. I teach, share skills, observe talents, provide advice, and listen to his continual chatter. As a role model, I give him my take on hard work and family loyalty. I see the influence I am having on him when I hear him repeating something I said or imitating something that I have done in the same way that I do.

For physical activity he likes to play tag, hide, and seek and ninja practice. We also go outside for neighborhood walks and races. I thrill at the opportunity to be his crony or playmate. When I'm tired, we spend time reading books, playing board games, cooking, and telling real or imagined tales.

I also play the unique role of wizard, and he becomes mesmerized by my life skills and stares wide-eyed asking, "How did you do that?" truly believing that only

I can bake cookies from scratch, heal a wound, or talk him out of a bad day, which delights me as some of the many blessings of grandparenting.

Finally, I also get to be his heroine. My grandson loves the fact that I always listen to him and am consistently available to provide super abundant power. He turns to me when he is carrying a burden and I try to serve as an emotional safety net to him since he is being raised by a single mom. He believes that grandmas can do anything anything, and I get to take pride in his confidence.

A U.S. fast growing phenomenon of 'grand families', which is a term defined as those grandparents who are providing significant care for grandchildren, includes all racial and ethnic groups. Recent Census based reports indicate that Native grandparents are three times more likely to be responsible for grandchildren in comparison to other ethnicities. According to the American Association of Retired Persons, some Native Tribal Nations, in the U.S., estimate up to 60% of children are living in homes where the grandparents are significant caregivers. At present, I provide care for my grandson seven days a week.

The cultural norm of elders and grandparents being held in high esteem is consistent in our Tribal Nations. Older adults are viewed as the ethnic transmitters, oral historians, and wisdom keepers. I get to pass on to my grandson all that makes me

Native and all that has allowed our people to survive. What I give to him, in addition to love comes walking, running driving, flying over miles and annals of Native history and folklore. What I say is so terribly important because he has become emotionally dependent on the words of his mother and me. So, I make sure that my words inspire, ignite, rekindle, provide a sense of wonder, and direction, desiring that they never dampen, condemn, or destroy. I am pleased to say that he is growing into a likeable, knowledgeable, kind, and caring young man. Building strong character in his life will be my undying legacy.

I don't allow the harvest of my life of hard work and dedication to darken into a winter of doubt in his life, because he deserves to see life innocently. Every day I get to watch him sprout into a new Native life, full of vibrant possibility and promise. Life has a way of slumping the shoulders, but when you look at my grandson, he stands tall.

Chapter 9
Mitakuye Oyasin: Circle of Life

"There are always loose ends in real life." Robert Galbraith

When I am not with my grandson, my life revolves around being a minister and a writer. My ministry has been a constant for me, but writing has been at times blocked and sporadic. There have been years between chapters and books. However, I marvel at my accomplishments as a writer of books bearing my name, and as a blogger, because both afford me a means to liberate pent-up experiences that need to be released. In retirement I have ample time to write, but during the time that it took to get to this point, I have been concerned about what will come next. I only foresee two books, or possibly three more, but what I do after theses is beyond me.

However, I have learned something valuable about the idea of waiting for my real life to begin. During the time that I have been writing, my sister has been diagnosed with cancer twice, my brother had an aneurism and my other sister struggles to manage her diabetes. My son has continual bouts with kidney stones, my daughter is a single mom, and my husband has had triple bypass heart surgery. And many of my family and friends have passed away. Subsequently, what I am learning is that while attempting to live and write, everyone else's lives have a dulling effect on mine.

Therefore, my life, like everyone else's is riddled with worries, hospital visits funerals, failed diets, heartbreaking news, disappointments, and goals unmet. Like anyone else's, it is complicated but worthy, loving but stressful, and blessed but disconcerting. Nevertheless, what matters most is that I am alive appreciating what

I have and what I can still do. I realize that some people are not endowed with the ability to burnish two words together, and even when the words flow, there is no electricity, but in transferring my thoughts to the printed page, I have been blessed.

However, everything has a way of working out because of the circle of life. And here is the point, from whence we start, we will always return. When I was a small child, my mother told me about the circle of life. She said, "Everything in life happens cyclically because each life circles and is part of the great circle." "The circle," she said, "represents the interconnectivity of all aspects of one's being, including a linking with the natural world and the world that is to come." Later, I learned about the medicine wheel, which is frequently believed to be the circle of awareness of the individual self; a circle of knowledge that provides the power we each have over our own lives.

Mother furthered, "The circle is a dominant symbol in nature and represents wholeness, completeness, and the fullness of life, including human communication. I am sure you have noticed how at our Native festivals; we sit together in a large circle." The Native talking circle is traditionally "opened" with a prayer and meditation. No one speaks until all have verbally acknowledged that they have completed their personal prayers. Mother also told me that, "When there is no break in the circle, it means that there will be continuous peace and prosperity."

Well, my life certainly has had its share of breaks. However, I've endured with a relative degree of prosperity and success. And I have withstood disconnection because mother introduced me to the healing circle. It is called *hocokah,* meaning sacred circle, which is also the word for altar. The hocokah consists of people who sit together talking, in prayer, in ceremony, and who are committed to helping one another and to each other's healing. I have never participated in this type of circle but have instead relied on the power of prayer directly to God. Knowing, however, that my people are steadfast in helping and healing each other, brings me a sense of pride. I pray for my tribe and our healing daily.

Musing of mother's words has given me much to consider. For example, the earth is round, the sun is round, and the planets are round. And when I was teaching several years ago, a student asked me why so many things in the solar system are round. I asked a professional scientific colleague for a standard answer, and he told me that the mutual gravitational attraction of the molecules pulls them into the shape that gets them as close to each other as possible: which is a sphere. His answer works fine for atmospheric bodies such as the Sun or Jupiter, but isn't so simple for other solid objects, such as rock formations.

However, he furthered that there is gravitational attraction acting between the rock's molecules, but for small rocks that force does not overcome the strength of the bonds holding those molecules in their relative positions. Since the strength of the gravitational force grows with the size of the object, a large enough rock will have a strong enough gravitational attraction to force formation into a round shape. I later deduced that even the universe supports mother's assertion.

Observing the natural world, animals often make their nests in a circle, supporting the premise that the circle is the basis of life. Even seasonal change is cyclical. And the life of humans forms a circle form childhood to adulthood and then back to a childlike state again. Mesmerizing is it not.

So, in my circle of life, I still have time before I become childlike again, and I love the fact that I've learned not to waste it. What I love most is that I am no longer a stranger to myself, or a partial person. And while my circle of life is nearing its end, I understand this, and fear not. Instead, I thank God for this life cycle every day, the one that mother explained to me so succinctly. And since honesty is the first chapter in the book of wisdom, I am now focused on the passions of my heart and striving to reach them, as I gradually circumvent my own circle of life.

Chapter 10
Lupan: Old Age

"In old age you are gently shoved off the stage and given a comfortable front stall as a spectator." Confucius

I believe that age brings intelligence, experience, wisdom, and a different type of beauty. So why are so many scared to grow old? Natives typically live to only our late sixties, or early seventies. So, we don't have to view those in our tribes as weather worn of wrinkled with age. The Bible says that even the mighty only get to the age of eighty, so, my time is nearing its end by both measures.

The United States is not a country for old men, or old women for that matter. Americans become taciturn and uptight when talking about sex but try talking about age. The vast majority will shove their heads in the sand about the fact that friends, family, and society at large is getting old. In the first half of 2020, life expectancy at birth for the total U.S. population was 77.8 years, declining by 1.0 year from 78.8 in 2019. For 2021, it was forecast that a third of all babies born in the past year are expected to reach 80. So, I still have some years of life to enjoy.

When I was young, I didn't think about getting old – I saw an old lady crossing the road, and never imagined that one day I was going to be her. I suddenly got to 60 and thought: 'I've got those spots on my hands that my grandmother had, I'm getting old', but by then there was nothing that I could do. I have found that what worried me when I was 40 doesn't worry me at 60. I wouldn't want to live to be 100. I'd be happy to get to the 80s. However, it's about the quality of life, not the quantity. I want to enjoy each and every day carefree and at peace, with the great peace. And I don't really care if people think I'm old – because in my mind I'm not."

No, I never worry about getting old, like women today. I've always had other things to worry about and was too busy planning for my future. My friends and I never talked about it, we just had great fun together. The worst thing about getting older I suppose is that I can't quite get around like I used to. Day to day, I play with my grandson, write my books, watch television, take naps, and sometimes share a meal with a friend, a lot of it more difficult than I ever could have imagined.

However, before I reached my golden years, I began reading literature about what I could expect in old age. A recent review from the Workplace Retirement Income Commission warned that millions of people face an uncertain "old age" thanks to cracks in the private sector pension provision. Last year, the Health

Service Ombudsman raised concerns that nearly a fifth of complaints received about the NHS related to care of the elderly, and a dossier containing stories about the alarmingly poor level of care elderly patients receive. My grandfather and father lived in nursing homes in their old age, and both begged to be taken out. Old people, these days, are forgotten, scorned, and abused. Well, that is not the life I want for me.

Nevertheless, I find it impossible to relate to these worrying facts, unable to face the reality that every day I am an inch closer to my own dotage. For me, getting old started at fifty, when my every day movements became more and more difficult, and my facial features began to sag. I became part of 'the elderly' the 'them', not the 'us', to such an extent that my advancing years provided a cloak of invisibility to my once productive and valued life.

I am not yet old enough to be offered a seat on the bus, and no one lets me in front of them in a queue, but not very often am I engaged in actual conversation with a person who is not family. Why even family make less and less time to engage me in everyday talk. I used to prefer scraping my tongue on sandpaper than engaging it in small talk with other people, now I avidly seek it.

For younger ones, it is easy to forget that I lived through the riots and civil rights law changes, or through a time when it was legal to fire a woman when she got married – or had a baby. But those times and experiences seem not to interest many today. My generation experienced the most tumultuous century in human history and yet at best we infantilize, or at worst, outright ignore the wisdom my generation gained from living through those historical changes. Pity instead of respect is what we are given. A 1998 study showed that younger people use baby talk (higher voices and simpler words) when communicating with people perceived as old. In fact, my daughter actually speaks more slowly and constantly tells me to write down what she says. She sees me as brainless, mindless, and disposable. I tell her she is rude, heartless, and callous.

On the other hand, I am certainly not forced to face up to my own ageing process because I am deftly airbrushed out of American society by an ageist media and a culture enthralled with youth. A survey by the Department for Work and Pensions concluded that "age related stereotypes in American society" identifies one in seven people as having a boss in their 70s and seeing this as "completely unacceptable." My father-in-law worked until he was 70 but fell one day at work and was forced to retire for fear of an age-related civil suit. He was told he was too old to cope in the workplace, not in touch with modern business technology, and simply no longer useful to the state agency where he was still actively contributing. Knowing his story, I stopped working at 57, long before anyone would say I was no longer useful and well under the age for any perceived civil suit threat.

However, one in three people in society is now aged over 50, and no one would know it by looking at how women are represented by the media. Take the landmark case of TV presenter Miriam O'Reilly, 55. After she was dropped from Countryfile in 2009, O'Reilly successfully sued the BBC for age discrimination. A BBC report commissioned following her case concluded that there was "particular concern" about the lack of older women represented on television, with more than a third of women over 55 saying there were too few of them. In trying to combat this, the BBC was accused of tokenism by Carole Walker, a 52-year-old newsreader who believes her subsequent appointment was "nothing more than a PR stunt," after she was given just one presenting shift in three months. It's not just the Beeb either – in 2008, Selina Scott, 60, won a payout and an apology from her job, after apparently being replaced in favor of a younger presenter. After hearing these cases, I wondered if I had waited too long to leave the workforce in my fifties.

Still, as an older woman, I see the media are problematic. Elderly women are viewed as overweight, sex starved or asexual. Even more damning, ageism in the media is particularly rife when it bisects sexism. Older men are still afforded a high media profile; just look at George Clooney, Tom Jones (on *The Voice*), Pierce Brosnan and Jeremy Paxman. However, once a man or a woman looses that youthful peek, we are overlooked.

A poll in 2011 revealed women feel they become 'invisible' at 46 and that our opinions no longer matter. A third admitted to being envious of how well their male partners were ageing. Being bombarded with advertisements with images of dewy teenagers selling everything from soft drinks to deodorant inevitably has a deep effect on my psyche. As I grow older, the inexorable march of wrinkles and grey hairs reminds me of my own waning power and pushes me deeper and deeper into oblivion. My own husband cackles at younger women before he considers taking a glance at me, and he has even said, "I am going to trade you in for two 30's."

Society has taught me not to see my own wisdom and experience but instead to see my aging as weakness and ugliness. So, when the inevitable truth of ageing confronts me in the mirror – is this sagging, or is that drooping? – I don't react well, especially when the ultimate compliment has become, "Oh, you don't look your age!" And it is not just women in their 30s fishing for compliments – figures released by The Harley Medical Group last year revealed that there has been a 17% increase in women over the age of 65 using age defying clinics and treatments. So, surely, age has become a disease, to be cured and eradicated.

There is, of course, the inescapable fact that the elderly remind others of mortality. I will admit that I am frightened of becoming weak and needy, of losing my mind and my mobility. A recent survey from the Disabled Living Foundation revealed that two-thirds of us dread becoming a burden on family and friends, while three in four fear illness in old age. The irony is that research has shown that those who have a positive view of ageing stay healthier longer. So, I am working on my positivity.

Those under 40 believe that to admit that they have anything in common with the aged, is to acknowledge that one day they will be like us. And recent research shows that people exaggerate the differences between themselves and others with characteristics that they fear having themselves.

Interestingly, in more 'collectivist' cultures – like Native American – it's this very reminder of mortality that underlies respect for and the value of the elderly. Our families know their time with us is limited, so we cherish each other – knowing that growing old is not growing obsolete, it is just taking on a new and more important role. Our nuclear society– where many of us have regular contact with grandparents – is very different from society at large.

It seems that shifting our attitudes towards ageing would not only be good for young people, but for us in our older age too. Studies show that for Natives, the prevalence of depression and dementia is far lower, implying that our culture may exert a protective influence on our elderly. Research in the Perspectives on Psychological Science Journal has shown that Natives get happier as we get older – when we move from middle to old age, when we focus on positive events and filter out bad ones, and cope with a negative event by shrugging it off and moving on. So instead of gasping at every grey hair, I have learned to celebrate my old age, delight in the innate self-confidence that comes with it, and to see it as a new stage of life rather than a slow march towards the end of it all. My life is good, because when I look around the world, I still see myself in it.

Nowadays I feel younger on the inside than I look on the outside. I certainly don't like looking in the mirror though, because I can't see properly to put on my make-up. I still like to look nice even though the only person I may see during the day is my grandson. Just because I'm older, I still want to look my best.

Nonetheless, getting older is frustrating. People don't take an interest in me. I think young people today don't have any respect for the elderly; they don't seem to have any sympathy for us either. I can't get out very much, can't read like I used to, and exercise sparingly. Also, I keep tripping and falling, feeling like my body is giving up on me. But I refuse to give up on myself. And I sure won't give in to youthful ignorance.

Chapter 11
Kiksuyapi Heyii: What Happened to My Memory

"Memories, even your most precious ones, fade surprisingly quickly."
Kazuo Ishiguro

I will tell you this though, I do have memory loss. It started with me simply forgetting names. Then it progressed to not remembering the route to frequently visited friend's houses. Of course I began to worry that my forgetfulness might be a sign of something serious, like Alzheimer's disease or another form of dementia. But I know that such brain freezes happen to most of us, in different degrees, as we age. Even experienced public speakers have their "Oops" moments, when a word or term they use daily simply refuses to come to mind.

My reoccurring memory loss manifests mostly in me not remembering where I left my keys. So, I am countering normal memory lapses by improving mental focus. I read and write daily to exercise my brain. However, my memory is completely at the mercy of time. I also physically exercise. Studies have shown that people who exercise, socialize regularly, and eat a healthy diet can minimize memory loss. So, I walk at least three times a week for 30 minutes or more and communicate with friends and family throughout the day.

The brain is always sweeping out older memories to make room for new ones. The more time that passes between an experience, the more likely I am to forget much of it. And while it is typically easy to remember what I did over the past several hours, recalling events and activities a month, or a year earlier, is considerably more difficult. This basic "use-it-or-lose-it" feature of memory, called transience is normal at all ages, not just among older adults.

Other studies show that events discussed, pondered, recorded, or rehearsed are recalled in the most detail and for the longest periods of time. Consequently, one of the best ways to remember events and experiences — whether every day or life changing — is to talk or think about them. When people approach 40, career pressures escalate, and the memory is more taxed. Those high stress levels were damaging to my confidence and memory. Later in middle age, with ever-increasing workloads, and multiple projects and responsibilities and deadlines and demands - my cognitive powers further diminished. I had to be on the internet, answer email, and respond to social media which conspired to destroy my concentration.

My changes included a drop-in brain volume, loss of myelin integrity, the thinning of cortical passages, impaired receptor binding and signaling, as well as altered concentrations of various brain metabolites. The accumulation of neuro-fibrillary tangles, often associated with Alzheimer's, has been diagnosed as normal ageing, but I worry that some of these areas will soon become my concerns.

When I retired to Puerto Rico, I found out how much harder it is to learn a new language as an older person. I now find it difficult to remember English words, let alone those in Spanish. I had a blind spot around the word "diminutive" for quite a while. I just couldn't say it. I couldn't remember how to say it.

Sadly, I know I will experience more frustrations and embarrassments and irritations as time goes on. Along with my hair, mental acuity is going too. Roll on anecdotage. The better news is that I read somewhere that mid-life moderate drinkers have been found to be less likely to develop cognitive impairment in old age than either teetotalers or heavy drinkers. So, now I have a drink every so often. I can't say that it helps, but it sooths my mind.

You may be asking what I am worrying about. I don't have Alzheimer's or Parkinson's or any reason to be worried about those diseases. My favorite novelist, Penelope Fitzgerald, was nearly 80 when her last and best book, The Blue Flower, was published. The singer Harry Belafonte is still sharp as a razor, and he'll be 96 on his next birthday. So are Bob Barker and Queen Elizabeth. William Wordsworth wrote: *And yet the wiser mind; Mourns less for what age takes away; than what it leaves behind.* Therefore, I wisely accept my aging.

I think Wordsworth meant that we should focus on the positives and accentuate our strengths. And I know that creativity is possible at any age. While I've given up trying to remember all the facts, I do continue to write, and my friends come to me for advice because they say that I can still see the bigger picture. Thanks to experience, I understand the patterns and trends of living. I can honestly say that wisdom is not what is known, it's how you interpret what you see. Wisdom is surely not based on memory, but life application.

Hence, I am no longer distracted by the details of life, but am amazed at how much I do recall. As I continue to write, my memories and observations are not always waiting for me but have to be drawn up. There is not a powerful relentless army of them, just beyond the mountain of my past resistance, but given time, they come back to my mind. And I try to make the logic of my life flow freely. I want to believe that I am a very smart aging lady who will never apologize for dreaming the most formulaic dreams about sunshine and romantic endings and so-long-as-we-both-shall-live sentiments. That is what aging teaches me and that is my story, and I am sticking to it.

Chapter 12
Maza Ska Beso: Mixing My Finances with My Children

"Mixing the family finances just becomes one big money mess."
Jean Chanski

When I retired, I put my bank accounts and other financial obligations in the name of my daughter as well as myself. As a mother, I talked to her about how to care for me before any situation turns into a crisis. She will be responsible for my long-term care, with a health care proxy and living will in place. Should I become incapacitated, my daughter will have to combine her role of single mother to include daily caregiver and major decision-maker for me. I know it will be hard for her to care for me, especially since I have never asked for help from anyone, but on the other hand, I know I can fully trust her. Also, my stern attitude is already being magnified the older I get, so she is surely going to have her hands full. She knows that I don't want a funeral and that I am still undecided about burial or cremation, but we will have that conversation soon too.

I've asked my aged sisters to help support my daughter if she might need. She has proven to be a pretty resources individual, and I don't think she will require any assistance, but life is changeable, and I don't want her to think that whatever happens might leave her in emotional or financial deficit, so I've talked to my son too. I have informed her that she may be able to take me on as a dependent on her tax return, if she ends up paying for more than half of my well-being, such as rent, nursing home care, food, or the like.

Currently, my daughter and I enjoy getting together for coffee. If something happens to me, the change in our relationship will be monumental for both of us. We are friends, as well as family. Like many children thrust into the role of observing the possess of my aging, we already struggle with boundaries. Preparing for what is eminent, will be physically and emotionally exhausting for her. And since I never establish close friendships, preferring self-sufficiency to intimacy, my daughter will endure the brunt of my frustrations and resentments, even more so as I begin to lose the ability to control the direction of my life.

So far, I am in balance. However, my personality exacerbates her feelings; she understands that her own reactions are often unfounded and unfair. At times, we both want to scream, but we know that slowly I am going to need her more. The truth is we have to remember that I am no longer independent physically or mentally. It's a truth neither of us want to admit.

According to Seattle geriatric internist Dr. Elizabeth Kiyasu, watching parents lose their independence is one of the most challenging realities of life. Children have witnessed parents' decision making their whole lives, important decisions about life, their children, and themselves. Then, without forewarning their decision making becomes impaired and children end up making decisions for them. Even if we rarely doubt ourselves when making decisions for our own children, making decisions while caring for elderly parents remains inherently ambiguous. Many times, I just don't want to make a decision and I ask my daughter to make the decision for me. My eating is a perfect example. If a child isn't eating, a parent simply insists that they eat for nutrition alone. But when I **refuse to eat,** a complex conversation often arises because she wants to keep me healthy for as long as is possible, and I want to keep my independence.

We've had some candid conversations about choices. The more often these conversations occur, the more prepared she becomes for my reactions. She tries to gauge whether or not I understand the consequences of the decisions I make, especially when they involve medication, finance, or advanced directives. I plan to establish Power of Attorney for my daughter, another valuable change in our legal relationship.

I have a strong emotional connection to her; stronger than I would to a stranger who is an aide or a nurse in an assisted living facility. Knowing that she will always be there for me, makes me happier. When all is quietly understood, fewer words are necessary. Sons are a blessing, but daughters are a special gift. And when I focus on my aging, observing my true sentiments without judging myself or overreacting, I perceive my extended well-being through her.

Chapter 13
Wichasha Wakan: Illness

*"Sometimes I think illness sits inside every person, waiting for the right
moment to bloom." Gillian Flynn*

It is true that I have been fortunate thus far, but ailments in later life are una-

voidable. However, there are many ways to keep our bodies healthy longer. While

there's nothing we can do about some factors - such as the genes we inherit from our

parents - there are steps we can take to minimize the risk of a painful and disabling

old age. I've looked at five age-related ailments and diseases and learned how to cut

the chances of them developing in me. Many of my preventative strategies - not

smoking, eating, and drinking healthily, exercising, and watching my weight - offer

protection against a range of serious health conditions.

Since I live on a tropical island, I take care when in the sun to reduce the risk of

skin cancer. I stay in the shade between 11 and 3, cover up when possible; use sun-

glasses with standard UV protection, a wide-brimmed hat and broad-spectrum sun-

screen, with an SPF of at least 70; applied liberally and often.

I have also taken part in national screening programs for healthy aging. My last

screening detected demyelination of my brain ventricles, making me more aware of my sensitivity to touch and the speeding up of my memory loss. Knowing why my body is breaking down, helps me understand and not fear aging.

As a Native, I am genetically more prone to heart disease, diabetes, alcoholism, myopathy, and early death. Knowing this, I don't smoke, even though both of my parents did, because it damages the arteries, and quitting is the single hardest thing to do. I exercise regularly because it reportedly lowers the risk of heart disease and stroke. I struggle to maintain a healthy weight, since being overweight can contribute to heart disease.

I've adopted structured weight loss programs of diet and exercise, supported by health professionals, and have lost about 5-10% of my body weight within six months - enough to reduce my chance of getting heart disease. Also knowing that excess alcohol use raises the risk of heart problems, I rarely drink. My father and my brother became functional alcoholics and I have always hated how they lived their lives and broke down more rapidly in their later lives.

I have researched my chance of developing cardiovascular disease over the next ten years. Natives are at high risk, so I've made further lifestyle changes. Diabetes, caused by too much glucose in the blood, can lead to serious health problems like heart disease, stroke, nerve damage, eye, and foot problems. My grandfather died with both of his feet cut off, as did my father. My sisters both have diabetes, with one on needle injections, and my brother has chronic problems with his feet. As for me, I am so far diabetes free, but never without concern that it will creep into my life. My eyesight is weakening, probably due to natural aging, but it too is a symptom of diabetes. However, at this point in my life, I chose not to be worried about what might be. Better to live each day in gratitude and with grace. And while I have sometimes moved through unforgiving waters, the point is, I am still moving.

Chapter 14
Colapi Cola: Seeing Through the Eyes of Others

"The truth is that if you know who you are and what makes you happy, it doesn't matter how others see you." Wendy Maas

The stereotypes, discrimination, and devaluing of the elderly seen in ageism, have significant effects on my aging, self-esteem, emotional well-being, and behavior. How people perceive the aging process varies greatly among cultures. Natives have great respect for the aged, especially our women. However, "ageism" is a common form of discrimination in the United States and in other societies.

The term ageism was coined in 1969 by Robert Neil Butler to describe discrimination against seniors and operates similarly to the way sexism and racism operate.

Butler defined ageism as a combination of three connected elements: prejudicial attitudes toward older people, old age, and the aging process; *discriminatory practices* against older people; and *institutional practices and policies* that perpetuate stereotypes about the elderly.

Because of the phenomenon, assisted living facilities now allow the elderly to keep a sense of independence while providing care and supervision necessary to stay safe. While countries like the United States and Japan focus more on independent care, the Native culture places greater emphasis on respect and family care for the elderly.

Along with ageism, in the United States, it is normal to view death as permanent loss and something to be feared, as opposed to a natural or tranquil transition. Depending on cultural norms, beliefs, and standards, aging can be an undesirable phase of life, reducing beauty and bringing one closer to death, not as an accumulation of wisdom, a mark of survival, and a status worthy of respect.

Research on age-related attitudes in the United States consistently finds that negative attitudes exceed positive attitudes toward older people because of the focus on looks and behavior. In his study *Aging and Old Age,* Posner discovered "resentment and disdain of older people" in American society. After repeatedly hearing the stereotype that older people are useless, I don't want to feel like a dependent, non-contributing members of society.

However, studies have shown that when older people hear these stereotypes about their supposed incompetence and uselessness, they perform worse on measures of competence and memory; in effect, the stereotypes become self-fulfilling prophecy. According to Cox, Abramson, Devine, and Hollon, old age presents a risk factor for depression caused by such prejudice. When people are prejudiced against the elderly and then become old themselves, their anti-elderly prejudice turns inward, causing depression. Research has found that people who hold more ageist attitudes or negative age-related stereotypes are more likely to face higher rates of depression as they get older. Old age depression results in the over-65 population, creating one of the highest rates of suicide. When I was about 40, and my father about 70, all he kept saying to me is, "Nance, don't get old." And he was also depressed a great deal of his time.

It has been observed that globally the elderly consume the most health expenditures out of any other age group. Traditionally, elderly care has been the responsibility of immediate family members or by the extended family. Increasingly in U.S. society, elderly care is provided by state or charitable institutions. Nearly one million elderly citizens are helped by assisted living facilities. These facilities allow the elderly to keep a sense of independence while providing care and supervision necessary to staying safe. In fact, elderly care in the United States is often viewed as a burden by family members who are busy living their own lives, making assisted living and respite care facilities a commonly chosen alternative. My brother lives in one right now.

In China, several studies have noted the attitude of filial piety, or deference and respect for one's parents and ancestors in all things, as defining all other virtues. Generally, people perceive death, whether their own or that of others, based on the values of their culture. People in the United States tend to have strong resistance to the idea of their own death and strong emotional reactions to loss through the death of loved ones. Viewing death as a loss and something to be feared, as opposed to a natural or tranquil transition, is often considered normal.

I know that I am nearing death, but Natives understand who we are - we know where we came from – and we accept our cycle of life, even though traditional beliefs have no way of being measured. We understand death, as a sphere with four stages: Birth, Life, Death, and the Afterlife.

Each Native is born a spirit, given a sacred name, adopted into a clan or nation, and recognized for specific gifts or talents. This thinking helps us understand our purpose on earth and our eventual destination when our spirit leaves the earth. Our challenge is to find the Creator, celebrate the Creator and be of service with our gifts to our people, to all of humankind, and to all Creation. We accept failures, confront our weaknesses, embrace healing and spiritual training through lodges, societies, and ceremonies of the nation. The nature of spiritual training imprints the identity of the person through adulthood and into our elder years.

When we are dying, we call for ceremonies, medicine and prayers that will guide our spirit to peace. My people believe that the spirit can be seen and felt leaving the body, traveling westward across the prairie grass, over a river and into the mountains. It ascends the mountains to the high clouds where a bright light guides it to the place where loved ones wait to embrace it. The spirit lives forever. It takes its place in the spirit world according to deeds completed on earth. We say that the Cycle of Life is complete when the spirit returns to its place of origin.

Both of the tribes that I am from use the Pipe Ceremony when one of our members dies. A medicine bundle containing a pipe and other sacred items is brought to the bedside of the dying person. Sacred tobacco and offerings of food and cloth are essential to the ceremony. The dying person repents or makes right his relationship with the Creator. The Pipe and the Bowl represents the woman, the Stem represents the man when they are brought together, life unfolds. Sacred tobacco is smoked in the pipe. Each time the pipe is raised, it is a celebration of life and all creation under the Creator. Creator's guidance is requested to join in. And any messages received through the pipe ceremony can be shared.

After the person dies, and when the person is born, Grandmother Moon obtains some of their hair. This is the sign that someone has died in the lower world and has begun journeying to Sky World. Hair is weaved into a mantle. Birth and death are connected since Grandmother Moon has domain over the fertility of women and when children are born and of course when someone dies.

Each person has a clan derived from their mother. Tradition reflects the duality of the world, male/female, light/dark, good/bad. When a person dies, the world is divided in two: people whose minds are grieving or clouded and clear-minded ones, such as family and friends. So, if death were to come to me tomorrow, I would be one of the clear-eyed ones with no fear. Because of this knowledge, many say that in my old age, my smile is like the blaze of a lantern. I am as Native as the light that emanates from the sun, or as my people would say or as strongly as the blue light that is found in the heart of a flame, and I will continue to smile and shine, right up to my death. I have no fear of dying, because death in my culture is the same as traveling my journey and doing the one thing that I can, which is to pass through it. Because of what my Native mother taught me, I can be as happy as any person alive, even as I age.

Chapter 15
Sicha Wana: Empty and Sad

"It was not the feeling of completeness I so needed, but the feeling of not being empty." Jonathan Foer

Of all the emotions that I have experienced in my elder years, feeling empty is one of the most uncomfortable. To feel empty is to feel incomplete. It's a feeling of something absent or missing inside, of being different, set apart, alone, lacking, being numb. It started when my husband left me, and then magnified when my daughter married. I knew about the empty nest and I was prepared for it, but the empty hole in my heart was not expected.

This feeling drove me to a myriad of unhealthy choices, like overeating, cynicism, over-shopping, and oversleeping. The feeling gradually and quietly eroded my joy, energy, and confidence. It flew under the radar and carried a tremendous power, while degrading my quality of life.

Just as every feeling tells us something about ourselves, so also does emptiness. I was lacking something vital in myself, something that is required for happiness and fulfillment. After a while I realized what I was missing: Emotion.

I began talking with scores of people who had the feeling of emptiness, and I think for me I have identified its cause. What happens in our childhood remains with us for a lifetime. For me it started with Childhood Emotional Neglect. Each of the people I spoke to grew up in a home in which emotions were not accepted, responded to, or validated. For me, it started when I was born and my mother did not want to take me home from the hospital, because she and my father wanted a boy. As the third girl in a family that needed tribal and social validation by having the man-child to carry the family name and our tribal traditions, I was ignored and flouted emotional neglect.

When my brother came home, born only thirteen months after me, I took myself off of the bottle. I did not want to eat like a baby since there was a new baby to feed. I tried to stop wearing diapers, but for over three years after his birth I peed the bed. My sisters and I shared a bed, so they were not only disgusted every morning when we all got up wet, but they actually treated me with disdain for years. I still hear them talking about my bed wetting days, and I am now in my elder years. Emptiness most definitely started then.

As an adult, when I feel empty, what is missing in me is the same ingredient that was missing in my childhood: acceptance, responsiveness, and validation of my emotions. But now, in old age, it is not from my parents that I need acceptance, it is from myself.

The strange and uncomfortable sensation is sometimes momentary, situational, and other times, long-lasting. When it overtakes me, I feel confused and upset. As I grow older, it consumes me with no apparent end in sight. When I am most empty, I digress into contemplating unresolved past incidents, and wallow in self-pity. I try to understand my emptiness, but it is often so intense and consuming that it leaps out at me like an image from a black and white photograph---concentrated, binding, extreme and often prophetic. However, studying it gives me an opportunity to meditate on its importance in my life. I have worked my whole life attempting to win the honor and respect of my family and friends.

I realize that there is emptiness and then there is emptiness; but for me, I can forget the pain that caused my emptiness, or the need to bring my family and friends honor, because in my old age, there are many blessings and the gifts that I can better reflect on. Finer that I sift through the sands and find the deeper boons, not the holes, and enjoy the pleasures that have filled my life. So, now on my face is a warm gradient smile, the kind that welcomes others into the grief-stricken folds of years of timeless emptiness, one radiating with joy and power.

Chapter 16
Le Mita Colapi: True Companionship from Whom?

"Many people will walk in and out of your life, but only true friends will leave footprints in your heart." Eleanor Roosevelt

This story would not be complete without giving a shout out to my good and trusted friends. A new study suggests that friendship is a significant factor in overall health and well-being. According to a recently published report in the Archives of Internal Medicine, having friends after 60 is linked to a longer life with personal utility. Being with others, is necessary to sustaining life. Family is one thing, but friendship is quite the compliment.

Since I'm post sixty and all the channels of friendship seem to have evaporated, I've become creative with making friends. I use my fine-tuned smile, because a smile illuminates a room like a pilot light and creates an atmosphere of possibility. It has worked for me throughout my life and is still working for me now.

Developing friendships was easy when I was in school. Everyone was the same age, lived in the same place, and the fishing pond was filled with people with whom I shared interests and values. And then I got through college and graduated. Many of the friends from yesteryear have long since left my friend pool.

What comes next is a hodge-podge: I've collected friends from different parts of my life. I became friends with the people at work -- again, a pool of people with common interests if not common ages. And I've become friends with neighbors -- people who generally match my age and socio-economic status.

When I became a parent, friendships were formed with other parents. I met them on my kids' sports teams, at school, and at enrichment classes I signed them up for, like basketball, piano, and ballet. But then the kids grow up and much of what I had in common with many of those friends – and my children -- disappeared.

What I am left with is a void with no easy way to fill it. What do I do to make friends now? Where do I find men and women and couples to hang out with when my own old friends are scattered to the wind? Skype, FaceTime and other social media keep me in contact with my long-distance old friends, but they aren't around to grab a cup of coffee with or go hiking with on Sunday morning. So, my friend pool is limited.

Making friend is critical to my overall happiness. Barbra Streisand had it right: People who need people are the happiest people, and I don't think Babs was talking about virtual friends. We need people around us -- brick and mortar friends to go out to dinner with, catch a movie with, join the new pilates class with, and the friendship cannot stop at worshipping together, because now that is done virtually too.

I made a specific prayer the other day to God, asking for a woman my age, with my interests, willing to have weekly discussions with me by phone and wanting to become my friend, and low and behold, I contacted a woman who is becoming my telephone buddy. When this shelter in place is finally over, I will be looking forward to spending quality time with her. She seems to really like me, and I surely like her. So, yes, I am making friends in my later years. And they will become true friends, because **only a true friend helps you pick up the pieces of shattered dreams, and then helps you create new ones.**

Chapter 17
Maka Sichu Schila Yata: To the Nursing Home

"Like most social institutions, it is usually impossible to pinpoint the reason or the source." J. Thomas Lamont

There is no doubt that I am in the final quinto of the American population. Currently, 16% of the Americans are 65 years of age or older. From a demographic point of view, the population is "twice as old" as the world population, whose proportion of senior citizens is 7%. According to forecasts, the proportion of senior citizens will reach 28% in 2050. Maybe I will be around to be a part of that statistic and maybe I won't.

Ageing is characterized by critical changes and turning points, such as the loss of a partner or a child, increasing health problems, the increasing need for care and possibly the move into a rehabilitation facility or a nursing home.

One study on residential facilities for the elderly confirms that residents often advise their family members against visiting them because they do not want their family members to see life as they have to live it. They lose their own self-respect because they are confronted daily with the increasing need for care. In principle the self-esteem of care residents appears to be based on social relationships, and the establishment of relationships among residents and staff.

I now realize that entry into a care facility constitutes a momentous and significant event and turning point in an elderly person's life. In fact, studies show that an ever-shortening life span of residents after their entry into the nursing home is noticeable. 22% of residents die within the first six months of being in a facility.

A human being's personality develops through social relationships. This means that identity develops via a process of social experiences, activities, stories, and dialogues with other people. Life situations and conversational partners change throughout the course of life, and therefore identity is seen as a constantly changing process. The formation of identity never ends. These changes include the alteration of living environment as well as bodily change.

I know that one day I may have to reside in a care facility. However, I don't want to live with bad conditions. So, I have arranged everything in the case of the need for extensive care. In my preparation for critical care moments, the move into a facility will cause too many changes, such as social status, impact on autonomy, feelings of having no place to call home, change in social contacts, and the reduction of activities that form my identity. So, for, as long as is possible, I have made provisions to stay in my home, or in the home of a family member.

And since I am a private person, I will always need a private space. My life as it is, is how I want it to remain. I don't want to place my dignity in danger. I don't want anything in my life to change. So, I am striving to focus on my ability to lead an autonomous, independent life. The freedoms that I now enjoy, I plan to keep right up to my time of death. In doing so, I will keep personal integrity, self-assertiveness, and personal freedom, by preserving clear boundaries that are characterized by my life at home.

I am a home body and will not do well in a care facility. I write these thoughts with full sanity, projecting that my normality will be to continue as close as possible to my current lifestyle. My life is not yet at the full stop or the end of a sentence, and I do not, at this time, see that time near, nor am I ready to bring my activities to a permanent halt.

Chapter 18
Peta Oo-Oohey: Final Changes

"The best changes we have in our lives are the ones that give us a second chance"
Harrison Ford

The final stage of life is marked by a crisis between integrity and despair. Since I believe I have had a positive impact on the world, integrity resides in my heart. I want to keep feeling good about my life and what I can continue to do by supporting others. I don't want to only live for today, but I want to be a positive force for tomorrow.

A life-span theory regarding motivation maintains that as time horizons shrink, as they typically do with age, people become increasingly selective, investing greater resources into emotionally meaningful goals and activities. Growing older means confronting many psychological, emotional, and social issues that come with age.

I know that with increased dependency in the elder years, older adults become at risk of elder abuse, like when a caretaker intentionally deprives an older person of care or harms the person in their charge. Approximately one in ten older adults report being abused and number is higher in the cases of dementia or other limitation diseases. I haven't experienced elder abuse and surely don't want to, but I do want to make others aware of it.

Despite the increasing physical challenges of old age, many new assistive devices made especially for the home have enabled more old people to care for themselves and accomplish activities of daily living (ADL). Some examples of devices are a medical alert and safety system, shower seat (preventing the person from getting tired in the shower and falling), bed cane (offering support to those with unsteadiness getting in and out of bed), and ADL cuff (used with eating utensils for people with paralysis or hand weakness). Advances in this kind of technology offer increasing options for the elderly to continue functioning independently later in our lives. So far, I have none of these, but I am not adverse to using them if the need arises.

Elizabeth Kübler-Ross, who worked with the founders of hospice care, described the process of an individual accepting death through her theory of grief. She proposed five stages of grief in what became known as the Kübler-Ross Model: *denial, anger, bargaining, depression,* and *acceptance.*

Denial: People believe there must be some mistake. They pretend death isn't happening, perhaps living life as if nothing is wrong, or even telling people things are fine. Underneath this facade, however, is a great deal of fear and other emotions.

Anger: After people start to realize death is imminent, they become angry. They believe life is unfair and usually blame others (such as a higher power or doctors) for the feelings being experienced.

Bargaining: Once anger subsides, fear sets in again. Now, however, people plead with life or a higher power to give them more time, to let them accomplish just one more goal, or for some other request.

Depression: The realization that death is near sets in, and people become extremely sad. They may isolate themselves, contemplate suicide, or otherwise refuse to live life. Motivation is gone and the will to live disappears.

Acceptance: People realize that all forms of life, including the self, come to an end, and they accept that life ends They make peace with others around them, and make the most of the time they have remaining.

With the deaths of my parents, in-laws, and others, I experienced these stages, and now readily accept the concept of dying. The stages may not necessarily be linear, but in some cases, like with the death of my mom, some linger for many years. The more my mother defied death, the more I remained stuck in the denial phase. However, not facing death until the very end is an adaptive mechanism for coping. I hope that my daughter faces my death better than I faced my mom's. The difference between she and I, is that she talks about mine quite a bit, and has already prepared her four-year-old son that it will eventually come.

As for me, I have a smooth fluid grace, as I move with confidence toward my death—sure of my life accomplishments and my pending final sleep.

Chapter 19
Ohinyan Mani: Last Trips

"Before that final trip, there is one last lesson, and death will make it stick: Take it when you can." Bridget Kemmerer

Last year, my sister came to visit me, not anticipating that a ferry ride to my island home would end with her seriously bruising her knee. When she decided to take a trip to visit me — at 75, — I knew that there would be things she wouldn't be able to do. She came with her daughter and her granddaughter, so she was not alone. And really, if it had not rained when we were on the ferry, all would have been okay.

I purchased tickets to come by ferry to Culebra so that her family could move about freely, take pictures, as we made the last part of their trek to my island. We were sitting on the outside of the ferry, when it began to rain, and my sister fell. Not many spoke English on the small vessel, so those who saw what happened said, "*Aih bendito*, bless you," loudly.

Being too old to help her, and fearing for my own fall, she remained down until her daughter, who was carrying her own daughter came to the rescue. It was scary and I feared that my sister would have to go to the hospital once we got off. Her daughter got her to a seat, and there she stayed until we docked.

When we first disembarked, she had to sit on a bench or lean against a wall while we waited for my daughter to come to pick us up. She kept saying she was alright, but her face told another story. I felt a little guilty every time I looked at her, especially since we ended up waiting for as much as half an hour for my daughter to arrive and take us to my house, where we were able to assess the damage caused by the fall.

Once at my house, she said she was not going to let the fall stop her from enjoying her vacation, and like a full-fledged trooper, she did not. She kept saying she was alright, so we had dinner and allowed her to rest, The next day, wherever we went, we had to take a lot of breaks and I even found a branch that we fashioned as a walking stick.

After about three days of watching her wrench with pain, we got her to go to an emergency care facility. The doctor gave her pills for the pain and a shot of cortisone. She was better for one day, but back the pain came. We kept breaking up the time she spent on her feet with rest time, either at home or at the beach. The restful time spent together bolstered our family relationship. And because one of us was injured, the others of us circled around her. In fact, even with my sister in pain, we managed to have a great time.

As I recall that day on the ferry there is no doubt that my sister and I were among the oldest people there. One morning before breakfast, we joined a group of 60-somethings that were with us to discuss the fall, and for the rest of the week, exchanged winks and catchphrases every time we met, allusions to getting old. As a family, we talked at every meal, sat silent sometimes in each other's company, enjoyed the scenery, and lounged a lot as the time ambled past us.

At night, we had drinks and talked about unresolved issues from our messy adolescence, my messy singleness, my Jehovah Witness beliefs, our daughter's boyfriends, in a vastly more exciting way than we'd ever thought possible. Being together in our old age, even while one of us was in pain, was one of the best times in our lives. God was watching over us quietly from his dwelling place, as quietly as the smoke that rises from a burning fire or as the morning dew forms over an open sea. And our time together felt good to us, not too hot, nor too windy, just clean and recycled through the lungs of those of us together as a family.

Chapter 20
Hecheto Aloe: Immobility

"She felt trapped, but she didn't have to. The world is wide open and ready, waiting for us to escape the bed and live." C. M Stunich

Looking back on that vacation, made me value my mobility. My father and grandfather lost their legs to diabetes, all of which reminds me of what life could be like if I were to become immobile. The week spent with my incapacitated sister gave me food for thought. Since my father and grandfather had diabetes, the medical solution at that time was to take a leg whenever gangrene set in. It wasn't a great fix because both were confined to wheelchairs until they died.

There are many other issues that can affect mobility in aging process. In an article by Anthony Fulworm, he pointed out some of the problems and solutions for dealing with loved ones with mobility issues. He said that immobility is a disability. With immobility, multiple areas of the body are affected. The effects of immobility cannot be reversed, they can sometimes be minimized, but never alleviated. The common risk factors of immobility in the elderly are:

Musculature, Joints, and skeleton problems, Arthrisis, Osteoporosis, Fractures, Podiatric problems, Neurological issues, Stroke, Parkinson's disease, Cerebellar dysfunction, Neuopatheis, Heart, lung and circulation problems, Chronic coronary heart disease, Chronic obstructive lung disease, Severe heart failure, Peripheral vascular disorder, Cognitive, psychological, and sensory problems, Dementia, Depression, Fear and anxiety, pain, and impaired vision.

My father and grandfather has just about all of the above. As they continued to decline, they were on prolonged bedrest, with general weaknesses that culminated in reduced eating and finally death. Knowing my family history, I make sure that my daily routine includes exercise. I often increase the level of exercises starting small and escalating gradually. Exercising helps with circulation to keep my heart working well and promotes repair and healing where needed.

I also eat and drink healthily. Drinking water ensures adequate hydration. When certain activities are difficult or uncomfortable, I use aids to help, walking frames, rolling carts, walking sticks, ankle support, heel pads and the like. So far, I have not had to restructure my home for handrails or mobility stairs, but I will if I have to. Old age is not going to get the best of me, and I am going to do all that I can to keep all of my body parts functional right down to the end. My life plan now consists of getting from the end of one day to the start of the next. And it has been working just fine.

Chapter 21
Kte Ni: Not in the Grave

"I'm not afraid of death; I just don't want to be there when it happens"
Woody Allen

In my family, we don't really talk about death. But every now and then, we joke about it. For some reason, there is a running joke among my immediate family about how each of us will die. My brother and I say we will come home one day and find the decomposing body of the other on the couch--- a bizarre thing to crack jokes about. But it's also, in its own, ghoulish way, a bit of a fantasy — an affront to the way Americans tend to die in the 21st century, without ticking machines and tubes and round-the-clock care. In this joke, my brother's death is simple, quiet, and un-complicated---and at home. So is mine.

I joke about death because I am as terrified as the next person about having serious end-of-life conversations. I don't fear dying, just talking about it. Usually, I don't have to think much about dying because I have devoted my life to saving lives and have become accustomed to talking about hope, not mortality.

In September, Ezekiel Emanuel — an oncologist, bioethicist, and health-policy expert — wrote a powerful essay for The Atlantic about why he will no longer seek medical treatment after 75. He said, "Living too long is a failure. It renders many, if not disabled, then faltering and declining, a state that may not be worse than death but nonetheless deprived." At 75, Emanuel says, he will become a conscientious objector to life-extending work. "I will need a good reason to even visit the doctor and take any medical prueba or treatment, no matter how routine and painless. And that good reason is not 'It will prolong your life.' I will stop getting any regular preventive tests, screenings, or interventions. I will accept only palliative — not curative — treatments if I am suffering pain or other disability." Well, I feel the same as Emanuel. I don't want to hold on when death is knocking at my door. I don't want to prolong the agony of a slow death for my family.

The following month, Atul Gawande, a surgeon, published a book, Being Mortal: Medicine and What Matters in the End. He argued that his profession has done wonders for the living but is failing the dying. "Scientific advances," he said, "have turned the processes of aging and dying into medical experiments. And we in the medical world have proved alarmingly unprepared for it."

After months of readings these debates, I had an epiphany. The conversations aren't about death at all. "Death" is the word that confuses the conversation, that makes people too afraid, and too angry, and too frantic to keep talking. These conversations are really about autonomy. They are about what makes life worth living, and if, in keeping people alive for so long, we are consigning them to a fate worse than death.

When death comes quick and fast, there is no fight to remain autonomous. Two graphs near the beginning of Gawande's book help make clear how recently this tension developed. The first graph shows what life used to be like a century ago: moving along, steadily, until some horrific event happened. Maybe it is a disease, maybe it was a car accident, or some like fate. Whatever the event, death happened quickly. The second graph shows, sometimes years of care on a patient that is more than ready to die.

But aging makes the facilities, both mental and physical, weaker. The activities we enjoy and the ones we find core to our identity become more difficult to pursue. As I get older, I am losing the mastery I once had over the world around me, the admiration I once inspired in those I love. Simple tasks — driving, home, grocery shopping, preparing meals — is becoming harder. The things I want to do aren't always things I can do. Emanuel writes about the plight of his father, who had a heart attack followed with bypass surgery at 77. It was more difficult to do the things that defined his existence as he withered aging, not the surgery.

I don't want anyone to prolong the process of death for me. Research purports that half of people 80 and older have functional limitations, and a third of people 85 and older have Alzheimer's. And as for the remainder, they, stumble listlessly toward death.

So far, I am not demented, my mental functioning has not deteriorated, but my mental-processing speed, long-term memory, and problem-solving skills are slowing. Additionally, my distractibility has increased. I cannot focus and stay with a project as well as I could when I was young. I move slower and think slower too. And I am not necessarily capable of making the decisions that I used to. So, I already rely on family support.

Emanuel's argument suggests that, even as doctors learn more about extending life, they have not been able to improve the quality-of-life preceding death. And Gawande's book acknowledges that the body and the mind will break down. In fact, the second chapter, "Things Fall Apart," is devoted to the ways our bodies — from the color in our hair to the joints of our thumbs — diminish at the end of life.

He states that the brain shrinks an astonishing amount in the course of a normal lifetime, with the frontal sections that control memory and planning diminishing the fastest. "At the age of 30, the brain is a three-pound organ that barely fits inside the skull," Gawande writes. "By our seventies, gray-matter loss leaves almost an inch of spare room." This explains why falls can be so damaging for the elderly: their brain has a spare inch of space to get jostled around.

"Living too long is dangerous," he writes. "It renders many disabled, faltering and declining, a state that may be worse than death." I look at nursing homes — with their scheduled meals, constant supervision, adult diapers, wheelchair-bound residents, and depressing bingo nights and think I do not want that. I do not want to give up control over my own life, my ability to see the people. Instead, I want to see and do the things I want to do right up to my dying day. I do not want to live a life where I can't dress myself, where I'm not allowed to feed myself, where I'm barred from living any semblance of the life that I live right now.

Also, dying in America is expensive. The six percent of Medicare patients who die each year typically account for 27 to 30 percent of the program's annual health-care spending. During the last six months of life, the Dartmouth Atlas has found that the average Medicare patient spends 9.9 days in the hospital and 3.9 days in intensive care. Forty-two percent see 10 or more doctors.

In the U.S., something so costly typically forces constant conversations about cutbacks and trade-offs and balancing priorities. But with end-of-life care, the opposite tends to be true: we can't talk about the cost of dying because it sounds like a discussion about rationing. Taking cost into account feels callous and inappropriate in the context of death. In its place, is not a thoughtful approach towards end-of-life care, but a dumb default that pushes everyone —to doctors.

To be elderly means a fight of all kinds, requiring all kinds of strength and then to rise the next morning only to resume the unglamorous, necessary work of continuing to survive. What patients, and families experience is — more tests, more surgeries, and treatments, no matter the cost in pain and disability. So, I am placing my attention on the specter of the future. I have lived my life as a Native woman, placing an eternal seal upon my heart. Love is as strong as death, and devotion is as unyielding as the grave. So, as I near the end of my life journey, I know that my last minutes will be motionless except for the rise and fall of my chest and the blinking of my flooded eyes. My breathing will become shallower, but I will realize that my relationship with everyone that was a part of my life will be there with me right to the bitter end.

I am getting tired and when my final sleep arrives, it will be like being on a miraculous raft on which I will hoist myself peacefully. I have a marvelously weird tranquility, called the great peace---a secret to successful living, which is seeing the world as through the eyes of a child, loving with joyful abandon, and expecting noth-

ing in return. Oh yes, that is the great peace, and I will have it right through to my

death.

Works Cited:

Achebe, Chinua. Things Fall Apart. First published by Heinemann in 1958. Reading, UK: Heinemann, 1986.

Archer, Bill. Smoothing the way on a trip with an elderly parent.https://www.washingtonpost.com, 2015.

Becker, Joshua. Those Things by Which Get Embarrassed. www.becomingmini-malist.com/mbarress/July, 2012.

Bordewich, Fergus M. Killing the White Man's Indian. Reinventing Native Americans at the End of the Twentieth Century. New York: Doubleday, 1996.

Boundless. "How Culture and Society Impact the Elderly." *Boundless Psychology.* Boundless, 10 Aug. 2015. Retrieved 13 Aug. 2015 from www.boundless.com/psychology/textbooks/boundless.

Boundless. "Socioemotional Development in Late Adulthood." *Boundless Psychology*. Boundless, 10 Aug. 2015. Retrieved 13 Aug. 2015 from https://www.boundless.com/psychology/textbooks/boundless-psychology-textbook/human-development-14/aging-late-adulthood-412/socioemotional-development-in-late-adulthood-292-12827/

Brenoff, Ann. How Do You Make Friends Post 50? The Huffington Post, June, 2012.

Bulletin 52, no. 3. Washington, DC: Population Reference Bureau, October 1997. George Levine, ed., The Joy of Secularism. Princeton UP, 2011.

Census.gov/prod/.../c2010br-10 The American Indian and Alaska Native Population: 2010.

Del Pinal, Jorge, and Audrey Singer. "Generations of Diversity: Latinos in the United States," Population: 2010.

DeMoss, Nancy Leigh www.reviveourhearts.com/articles/lies-women-believe-about-unfufilled 2015

Erdrich, Louise. Tracks. New York: Harper and Row, 1989.

Fischer, Mary A. AARP, www.aarp.org › Health › Brain Health & Wellness August 1, 2012.

Gillory, Elizabeth. Women of Color: Mother-Daughter Relationships in 20th Century Literature.
University of Texas Press: 2005.

Hall, Mary. The Effect of Social Isolation and Loneliness on The Health of Older Women. www.pwhce.ca/effectSocialIsolation.htm 2013.

Hazen-Hammond, Susan. Timelines of Native American History. New York: Perigee Book, 2010.

Heilig, S. J. sitation.aip.org/content/aapt/.../1.3479713American Institution of Physics, 2010.

Hicks, Cheryl.www.theguardian.com › Lifestyle › Health & wellbeing The Guardian Loading.Jun

Hood, Spilka, Hunsberger, & Corsuch, 1996; McIntosh, Silver, & Wortman, 1993; Paloutzian, 1996; Samarel, 1991; Wortman & Park, 2008.

Huerta, Daniel. The Complete Guide to the First Five Years of Marriage, a Focus on the Family Book. New York: Tyndale House Publishers, 2006.

Indian Health Service. Disparities. Fact Sheets; 2017.

Kliff, Sarah. Americans Refusal to Talk About Death. www.vox.com., May 19, 2015

Lickus, Jay. Twitter: www.twitter.com/Survive_55, Retrieved August 13, 2015.

Moore, Debra. Being Overly Dependent Can Cause Problems. www.sacramentopsychology.com, *2011.*

Muché, Julie A. Geriatric Rehabilitation. www.agingcare.com/2008.

Mutchler, Jan. Grandparents Responsible for Grandchildren in Native-American

Families. Social Science Quarterly 88(4):990-1009, December, 2007.

New York Presbyterian. Aging and Loss of Independence. *www.cornellcares.org/pdf/handouts/gal*.

E. J. Porter and J. F. Clinton, "Adjusting to the nursing home," Western Journal of Nursing Research, vol. 14, no. 4, pp. 464–481, 1992.

Reviewjournal.com/.../transition-retirement. Las Vegas Review Journal.

Separation and divorce. Theravive.com/services/divorce-help .2015.

Singer, Jackie.wordpress.com/2012/11/30/a-divorce-ritual, Nov 30, 2012.

Solitto, Marlo.www.stylist.co.uk/life/why-we-are-scared-of-growing old.

Steffe, Marita. How We Can Accept Getting Old. *maritasteffe.com.* March 12, 2014.

Viveiros, Janet Aging in Every Place: Supportive Service Programs for High- and Low-Density Communities, March, 2014.

www.agingcare.com/Articles/what-it-feels-like-to-be-old-150011.htm.

www.aplaceformom.com. Resources. Apr 22, 2015.

www.Washington Post. com. Two Native American women are headed to Congress. November 8, 2018.

www.webmd.com/...aging/.../role-reversal-caregiving-for-aging. 2018

www.cpd.Utoronto.Indigenous Perspectives on Death and Dying Ian Anderson Continuing Education Program Ian Anderson Continuing Education Program in End- in End -of-Life Care Life Care, 2020.

Webb, Shelly. Immobility Problems and Solutions. http://www.brooksstairlifts.co.uk. September 30, 2011.